A Walkabout is a right of passage that the Australian Aborigines practiced. During a Walkabout a person would undergo a journey during adolescence and live in the wilderness for a period of time. It is known as a spiritual journey somebody takes as a transition into adulthood.

I came home one night to my parents furious with the decisions that I had been making. Within the next twenty-four hours I found myself stranded in the middle of the western desert of Utah with only the essentials of survival and a journal. It was my turn to experience the Australian Aborigines' "walkabout."

Copyright © 2009 by Steven Andrew Reynolds (Ven Rey/Ven Reynolds). The author retains sole copyright to his contributions to this book.

No part of this book may be reproduced, scanned or distributed in any printed or electronic form without permission. Please do not participate in or encourage piracy of copyrighted materials in violation of the author's rights. Purchase only authorized editions

ISBN 978-0-615-29084-3

Images provided by Outback Wilderness Expeditions

Cover Art/Design by Ven Reynolds

To my parents

Laura and Grady Reynolds

Without your intervention I don't know where I would be today. Maybe better off, maybe worse. All that I know is that I wouldn't have learned and been able to share this story. I know I've been a pain at times but thank you for everything you've done for me.

Also, everyone in the Dingoes my second time around!

Son,

We are writing this letter to help you better understand our reasons for whisking you away to wilderness camp. Though you may have been caught off-guard by our sudden action you were aware of our concerns about your change in behavior.

We were most concerned that you would back yourself into a corner where you felt your only option was to runaway from home and drop out of school. We love you beyond measure and we were fearful you would continue to make poor decisions that would most certainly have an extreme and negative impact on the richly rewarding life you deserve.

It broke our hearts to temporarily remove you from our home – we hurt, we cried, we still hurt and still cry. We did this because we love you and thought your best chance at a bright future required us to remove you from this environment and help you get a fresh start.

Over the course of the last eighteen months you have made choices and engaged in behaviors that have shocked us and run contrary to the responsible and loving person you had become.

You showed disdain for many of your teachers... your schoolwork became unimportant... you did not do the homework necessary to maintain good grades and did not attend several of your classes.

You lied about your plans and whereabouts... You defied our authority and rules. You obtained a tattoo when you were sixteen and concealed this from us for many months, though you proudly displayed your tattoo to your younger brother who kept your secret. You admitted to sneaking out of the house...

You have admitted to sneaking friends (boys and girls) into our house while we were traveling and you were under the care of your grandparents. You also admitted to drinking in our home.

You have engaged in risky and sometimes illegal behavior. You have admitted to promiscuous sex with both males and females. You have began to smoke cigarettes without shame – recently being ticketed by a school police officer while on the school premises.

Your only concern has become you. You have overtly and proudly used your charms to manipulate friends and loved ones. You use both anger and tears to intimidate or cause people to feel sorry for you – only to get your way. You threatened to runaway from home to manipulate our emotions and left home for a night when we didn't stop you.

We understand we have been less than perfect parents and role models... But, you cannot let our shortcomings justify your poor choices and behavior. You must make good decisions for your future happiness – not ours.

You are a very kind, caring, loyal and thoughtful son and friend... You are a confident, driven leader who is very focused, organized and responsible. You have unique insight that allows you to excel at both the arts and business...

You are an extremely gifted, talented and creative writer and a great photographer with very innovative, forward thinking. You have an eye for business – you know what it takes to make a business grow. To top it off, you were great at keeping your room and bathroom clean and took great care of yourself!

❊ ❊ ❊

Some of this letter has been condensed to fit the story. However, all of the points were conveyed. This letter was the first letter I received after being sent to the western desert of Utah. To my worst nightmare and darkest fear. To a place I struggled, a place where my lies grasp me and tear me apart. A place in the back of my mind that haunts me, even through the repression of those memories.

This is my confession and my story of my greatest fears. I didn't choose to physically go there and I resented my parents for that. But now, I am choosing to go back, to explore those fears, the hatred and the resentment in some minor hope of leaping over the greatest hurdle of my youth.

surviving steven

Day 1

Today is the first day; I'm still in disbelief. I'm somewhere west of Salt Lake City. Inches of snow cover the ground. Juniper trees have icicles hanging lifelessly from them. It's cold… very cold. The fire danced in the cold wind. I'm sitting by the fire trying to stay warm. I have several layers on. I swear this journal is the only thing I have to keep me sane.

My supplies are as follows: five changes of underwear, a pair of navy underwear thermals, a pair of beige thermals, five pairs of wool socks, a sleeping bag, an over bag, a large silver tarp, a green ground tarp, a hide of leather, wool pants, a bomber jacket, a fleece, a hoodie, waterproof boots, gloves, hobo mittens, cordage and a food bag.

My food: Macaroni noodles, rice, dehydrated beans, wheat flour, corn flour, corn meal, oats, germaid, brown sugar, powdered milk, powdered cheese, powdered butter, raisins, granola, shell-less sunflower seeds, a jar of peanut butter, two packets of tuna, two packages of ramen, an apple, an orange, a lime, a banana and spices (cinnamon, salt, pepper, Mrs. Dash, and baking powder). Oh and a small metal cup. Sounds delicious, right?

Today's goal: Make a wooden spoon so I can cook and eat warm food. How the fuck am I supposed to do that? I hate this place. I hate my parents. I hate the world. I hate these people. I don't belong here. I don't even know why I'm here. I'm suppose to get a letter from my parents, I think, explaining their reasoning… I wasn't *that* bad of a kid.

Sure I was more independent than most. Sure I lied to my parents, what teen doesn't? (Maybe it's because I told my parents I was gay.) Sure I rebelled against my parents to the point that I begged for them to kick me out. I wasn't going to be the one who left. More sympathy if I got kicked out rather than a "runaway." Right?

My brain is a scattered mess, always has been and still is. Deep breath, thirty days… or sixty. Or eight weeks. The timeframe keeps changing depending on the person I talk to. I'm still not so sure this is all real. Maybe I'm dreaming this. I knew places and programs like this existed, but was I a candidate for this extreme of a punishment?

That's what this feels like, a punishment. For being too independent. For hating my family. For being successful at such a young age. For being sexually active. For acting older than I am. It's a little disturbing.

I'm pretty sure Utah doesn't have laws protecting me as a minor. In Texas, at seventeen, they wouldn't legally be able to "capture" me and force me in a place like this… in Texas I was safe. I hate Texas. I have since we moved there on my tenth birthday. But Texas protected me and I never fully appreciated it until now.

My first assignment is to write a Life Story. My life story. While here at First Camp (that's what they call the first stage of the wilderness program. First Camp… I wonder how many camps there are.) Apparently this is the boring part; we just sit around and can't talk to the other students. Apparently we hike after we leave this.

Gah, I hate cardio. I mean I love to run it releases stress, but I'm a smoker and cardio is my worst enemy. Gasping for air after anything more than a brisk walk… no thanks.

I think I'll write my Life Story tomorrow. I'm going to sleep now… maybe this is all just a fucking nightmare.

Day 2

Fuck. I'm still here. It's not a dream...

Dear Diary (never thought I'd write *that*, but you know, whatever),

Today I made a bow drill set. A bow drill is used to make fire. Man make fire. Man cook food. Yeah, the primitive rubbing sticks together. It's actually harder than it may seem. Then you have to make a bow from the Juniper tree and tie cordage around it. You put a Sage Brush spindle (that I had to hand make with a knife) in the cordage and make a hole with it.

The friction between the Sage pieces creates a coal, and you take that coal and put it into a nest (made of tree bark). Blow on it softly until the nest catches fire and put it in the fire pit. Ven make fire. Ven cook food. The joys of relying on primitive survival skills. I also constructed a backpack from a Juniper tree. It sucks and isn't that stable, but whatever. It'll get the job done.

Oh how I dearly miss the city... McDonald's and Chick-fil-a... television... and a bed.

Today was sunny and warm (well, warm in the sense that the snow on the ground became kinda slushy, but not warm enough to melt the God damned ice). I sure do miss Texas and its glorious warm weather...

Well I guess this is where I start with my life story. I'll write it in here, for my eyes only, I think... They want me to share it, but my life has been pretty disappointing if you ask me. It's kinda sad and I hate it. But I have to write this if I ever want to get out of this God forsaken place.

My Life Story

I was born December Ninth 1990 in Tampa, Florida. I was a little more than eight pounds. I was a chunky baby. I was now the younger half-brother of my dad's child from a previous marriage. I don't know exactly in what order the events over the next two years occurred, all I know for sure is that my dad and mom separated and divorced a year after my birth. My dad won custody and soon after married the woman who would become my "other mommy." With the marriage I gained an older stepbrother.

The four of us lived in Florida, Oklahoma, and Texas. From what I know, we didn't have a lot of money and lived in apartments and with my grandparents often. In 1994, my new mom, gave birth to the youngest addition to our family, a baby boy.

We moved around often, not in one place more than two years, I think because of my dad's job. After second grade we moved to Wichita, Kansas. For the next year and a half I was happy. We lived in the first house my parents had ever owned, my dad had a very nice job, I had all the friends I could ever ask for and for once in my life I didn't feel different. I've always felt different. Here I left behind the image of a boy who played with dolls, who didn't like sports, who was "less of a boy" than others. For the first time, my friends were mainly other boys my age.

December ninth 2000 we moved to Plano, Texas. I had to leave behind the friends I had made. Entering school halfway through the year, I seemed left out. I didn't have the chance to make a lot of friends and because of that, the next year I didn't make that much more and that's when the rumors started.

By the time I was in middle school I was being bullied. I was heavily bullied. I was into theater, and very talented. People liked to push me a little, but mostly it was the whispers as I walked by that killed me. I had been labeled a "fag."

By the end of my sixth grade year I didn't know what to do, I felt abandoned and like everyone hated me. My first real girlfriend had a friend who tried to commit suicide by cutting her wrists. I tried. I couldn't do it though. Summer came and I didn't have to deal with the pain from my peers.

I immersed myself in Church, going twice a week every week. I got a lead in the church's student choir musical as the "Angel", my co-star was the "Devil." I preached the word of God non-stop, attended prayer warrior meetings and prayed that what was happening to me would end.

Seventh grade was even worse. I was isolated; I had very little friends, yet everyone knew who I was. Everybody talked about me. Rumors spread like wildfire. I was "gay" then I "got some girl pregnant" then I was "gay" again. The physical bullying got worse. The teachers saw it and felt so bad for me that when another student teased me, I punched him, the teachers simply said they didn't see anything.

The administrators, however, were not as helpful. They dismissed the sexual harassment issue by asking me if it was true. True or not, the students had no right to treat me that way. We had two weeks left of school and my parents withdrew me, threatening lawsuits.

I started my eighth grade year at another middle school. The rumors still hovered, but people left me alone and I made friends, mostly girls.

High school was a change of pace. While there are always going to be those select few, ignorant people, my life seemed to get better. With two others, I produced a documentary on high school cliques. I wrote a script based on bullying and filmed it my freshman year.

After putting all my blood, sweat and tears into the movie at age fifteen, I appeared on Good Morning Texas to talk about the movie. I also had several interviews because of my achievement. I was becoming a "Somebody".

The beginning of my sophomore year I met a guy who expressed an interest in me. Curious as to whether or not I was gay, I decided to pursue it. When my parents found out I immediately ceased communication with him and put an end to the whole thing.

At the same time, the editor of the film I made lost the footage and covered up his failure by blaming me for insufficient directing and refusing to hand over any footage. I quit acting, I quit writing, and I quit film.

Spring of my sophomore year revealed a new talent. Photography. I started charging and even got a job at a mall studio that summer, at age sixteen.

After my seventeenth birthday I began experimenting once more with my sexuality. New Years Eve I decided to have sex for the first time with a guy I just met and his boyfriend.

The next day I met another guy through a friend and invited him back to the house. We had a brief relationship based on cheating and lies. I experimented with ecstasy once during this time. I threatened to leave my unhappy family. I looked for apartments with my friend and planned on moving in with him and the previously mentioned guy.

I gave up on school; I hardly attended classes. I gave up on my writing and photography. I labeled myself "gay" and tried my hardest to live that lifestyle. I was unhappy and sometimes couldn't even look at myself in the mirror. I had suffered heartbreak after heartbreak.

That's all, my whole life story… that's how I perceive my life. Full of disappointments and failures. I'm not worth that much. I can't be worth that much if that's what my seventeen years has amounted to. I am numb and I don't think I'll ever forgive my parents for sending me to a therapeutic program where I have to relive all those past failures.

Day 5

So I'm not the best person to keep track of a journal. I probably won't write everyday. It's all I have out here though. But the days are short and I don't have a flashlight. I think the sun rises a little before nine and sets before six. Lots of time to sleep. That's the good thing about winter; maybe this time here will fly by because I'm sleeping so much?

Oh by the way I left first camp. Yesterday. And the next few hours were pretty eventful. I hiked about two miles, got to where we were going to set up camp and basically lost it. I watched as the staff members helped me unpack my belongings from my crappy backpack and decided I *have* to get out of this shit hole.

The staff and other students set up camp, digging a latrine, a sump, and a fire pit. I walked past my shelter, venturing towards the setting sun with only a water bottle and the clothes on my back. "I am going to get back to the city tonight", or so I thought.

It was a ridiculous notion to think I could walk nearly two hundred miles. Or even just the fifty to get back to the highway in one night. Especially in the snow with no food and only a bottle of water. But I'd kick myself forever if I didn't try.

And that I did, I got a whole three miles before getting caught by the staff members that were called via the emergency satellite phone (the satellite phone that the staff insists doesn't exist).

My thoughts during my venture across the three miles of vast desert were filled with fear and adrenaline. Apparently I could have died, but I wasn't scared of death, I welcomed it at this point in my life. I taunted it, "take me if you can." Because I felt immortal. I can't explain it; it was just an irrational thought that I believed. But everyone else was scared of my fate. Everyone except me. And I guess that's why I'm here.

When they caught me, one of the staff members took me into an empty opening and looked around, almost furiously and said, "Do you see that?" I shook my head with confusion. "Exactly. There is nowhere to go. No one around. Even if you were to stumble across someone, I promise you they won't be friendly. Ranchers and drunk rednecks with guns." Or something to that effect. He took me back to the car and we rode back to the campsite.

And at that moment I had officially been placed on "run watch." I was required to be in arms length of a staff member at all times, I couldn't use any sharps (knives, saws, machetes or even scissors). And to top it off I had to sleep in between two staff members, tucked in under a tarp… tightly tucked in.

I obviously couldn't sleep especially since I had to pee. But every time I got up, they were standing so close to me and it was so cold that I just couldn't go. I was miserable. Miserable and utterly alone. At least, I felt as if I were alone. The fifteen or so people in my group didn't seem real.

Nothing seems real, to be honest. I fucking hate this place and I just want to go home… no I have no home. I just want to leave and get as far away from this place as possible.

I have to read some books "LSD" (a.k.a. Leadership and Self-Deception, it's not a drug, it's a book. A very, very boring self-help book.)

Today we have staff exchange. We were blessed with the presence of three people who loved kids and the outdoors... yeah, whatever. The first was an elderly man with an aura of wilderness screaming from him. He was short and chubby with a gray beard... a long gray beard. He wore a snowcap on his head. He kinda resembled Santa Claus, except dirty. He was loud and obnoxious (who knew such a small man could pack so much noise and energy!) He was also abnormally strong. He carried two bluies (5 gallon water jugs, weighing about 40 pounds each) up the steep hill.

The second was a female staff. She was boyish in appearance and very quiet. She seemed a little shy. Maybe she could be my connection to the real world? Probably not, she looks like an outdoorsy person.

The third staff was a Jewish man. He reeked of onions and garlic. He was also short and had a little extra weight on him. Great... this next week is going to consist of a loud old man, a not so talkative girl, and a smelly man. And I get to sleep with them!! That's just the icing on the cake... oh what I would give for a piece of cake right now...

Day 8

Here's the 411. Staff changes out every week on Thursday. We get new food with the new staff. We hike Friday, Saturday, and Sunday. Therapy on Monday and Tuesday. Along with new food drop and laundry exchange. And again we hike on Wednesday. A very pretty schedule that we live for.

Food rationing sucks, we get tuna on Mondays and PB on Thursdays. I don't know how to cook much and I only take about half the food. We aren't allowed to food share or food trade because somehow the plastic baggies of untouched food can spread germs and illness. Get real. I take the macaroni noodles, the rice, oats, PB, all the dry foods (except the beans) and all the spices. Not much of a diet. Maybe I'll lose some weight, I noticed I put on a few pounds before arriving.

Still on run watch and can't use any of the sharps, meaning I can't do anything productive. So I guess I can stick to my journaling. It's what I'm good at and obviously all that I can do. I've read the book LSD and also filled out all the booklets they've given me. When it comes to work, I'm a very productive person. I can finish days of work in hours. I think I'm going to be bored a lot.

Today we are hiking... Yay! If I haven't mentioned it before, I fucking hate this place. It's utterly ridiculous and I can't stand the therapy crap they put us through! It's absurd. I'm still on run watch and I don't really talk to the other students. I just don't fit in. Like usual.

Tomorrow is my first official therapy day with my therapist. I met her briefly last week; I think she's got a stick up her ass. But whatever. I guess the only way to escape this torture is to comply with this bullshit.

Day 11

Another eventful night occurred. I left camp again, this time not because I ran away, but because of an illness. After the heart wrenching therapy session I was removed from being on watch and made my first shelter.

On Tuesdays the nurse comes around to all the groups (I belong to the Dingos) and checks up on everyone. She just missed the staff and student that left for the hospital when she paid us a visit. That night I contracted the same illness. Fuck the wilderness.

I was throwing up and had intense diarrhea... and by diarrhea I mean, "butt pee." It was like pissing out of my ass. As the night progressed I insisted that I had side pains (towards my appendix). Since appendicitis is deadly, they *had* to take me to a hospital. Even if it wasn't, their thoughts were "we better be safe than sorry." I knew this and even after the pain ceased I continued to pretend it hurt. That's how I ended up in the emergency room at 1:00 AM.

As we waited for tests they gave me a morphine drip to get rid of my nausea. On the way over they had to pull over so I could vomit. Yeah, hell. Anyway I'd only been out for two weeks but it felt so good to lie in a bed and read magazines. I got to read Entertainment Weekly and learned about the Oscars.

I prayed to a God that I no longer believed in. I prayed that I had appendicitis. I would be discharged from the program because of surgery and would go home... where I would then pack my bags and leave. However the blood work and tests came back normal.

Unfortunately, I was fine. That night we went back to the base of operations and slept. This morning I woke up and I was shipped back two hundred miles from civilization. At least I got to use a toilet as I got over the illness.

Of course, we had to hike. I made a makeshift pack that didn't hold well and struggled as we hiked. My pack was uncomfortable and I opted out of the group excursion of finding a top rock. A top rock is a soft rock used to hold the spindle in a bow drill set steady and it allows one to puts pressure on the spindle to create the friction necessary to create a coal. I pulled the excuse that I was sick (which was partially true).

We made camp an hour ago and I'm sitting in my shelter, about to go to sleep. I didn't feel like dinner and maybe tomorrow will bring more pleasure... though I doubt it. But we do get new staff!

Day 12

Today was pretty chill. A special staff came in and challenged us to hold a rock all day. If we lasted the whole day we get a special treat (a chocolate chip cookie)! So while holding my rock I began making my Possibles bag. A Possibles bag is a bag used in addition to our packs. It's used to store food for hiking and things like this journal.

I have a light colored hide of leather I'm using for the main parts and black for the sides. My bag is actually pretty cool. It's a whole lot more creative than any others that I have seen.

Day 14

This morning was a disaster! We set camp on a ridge and in the middle of the night a strong wind came through and destroyed everyone's shelter, even the staff's shelter! Of course, I built mine very sturdy and the wind only messed it up completely, while everyone else's was torn down.

After everybody got situated we had breakfast and I finished my Possibles bag. Throughout the entire breakfast one of the staff members would not shut up about how he "accidentally" got two jars of PB in his food drop.

Okay so you're probably thinking, so what, it's just peanut butter, but out here in the wilderness the most important items to someone are their PB jars, their granola, their brown sugar, and their sleeping bag. When someone gets an extra amount of any of those items, they better watch over it very carefully!

Anyway, as everyone scattered away, I noticed the staff member left his food bag and the extra jar of peanut butter was just lying there in the dirt. The delicious jar of unopened peanut butter seriously was calling my name. So I did the right thing and walked away.

Once I got to my shelter, I realized that "hey… you're almost out of PB and he doesn't need that! He gets to leave in a week and he can eat all of the PB he wants!" So I ventured back to main camp and there it was, just calling for me to take it.

Slyly, I slipped it into my coat and went back to my shelter to pack my things. I quickly ate the remaining amount of PB I had and threw the peanut butter jar in the trash. When I went back to camp, the staff noticed his missing PB and the staff began searching everyone's belongings.

I quickly went back to my shelter and threw the jar as far as I could into the snow. Then I realized, bad idea. I could see the staff sorting through the belongings of whom he believed actually took the PB. I pretended to pee, in case he could see me and I ran to get it, and put the jar in my Possibles bag.

After everyone's things were searched, the dumb ass staff member said he saw tracks in the snow by the other kids' shelter (very close to mine as well) but with no evidence, he could prove who did it (even though the blame was not focused on me). I ate that peanut

butter with such delight that it was sickening. I even ate it on the hike in front of that staff, just thinking to myself what a dumb ass he was.

When we got to camp they did another search... still nothing. I was very sly and very proud of myself today. Now I'm sitting in my shelter, trying to go to sleep. I skipped out on tonight's gathering (I'm pretty sure I haven't been to any).

Day 16

Today our staff found a "message in a bottle". The staff member, a young man in his twenties, kind of a hippie with his shaggy blonde hair and kind of dumb, brought it to us. He seemed like a major stoner. The other staff was the loud old man, his nickname, Buzz.

The blonde staff said he saw it poking out of an anthill. It was an old Coca-cola bottle with a small piece of paper stuffed inside. The paper was closed on both ends with shotgun shells. The staff passed the paper to another student. The student opened it and read it out loud. "I loved and then lost. I lied and still lost. Yet no matter how many regrets you burn, the pain of the coals are still there. Only ashes blow away in the wind."

The staff wanted to focus on the negative aspects of the quote. About how lying causes nothing but loss. They made a point that if you forgive the pain will go away, not just the "ashes" (or surface wounds). Which is a nice dream, if that can actually happen. As far as I know true forgiveness is impossible. You will always have that feeling of resentment towards someone who has wronged you, no matter what they do or say to change it. The staff really pissed me off when I expressed my opinion. My usual optimism seemed to be left back in Texas and so I simply said that the quote was right.

To me, the quote means, no matter if you honestly love yourself or others the pain will hurt the same as if you deceive yourself or others. Even if true forgiveness is possible, and you can let go or "burn" away those negative feelings, the scar will never disappear all the way. There will always be that reminder of the pain you endured. And if hurt again, that scar will open up as if the stitches never healed the wound.

A memory came to my mind when I read this, but I didn't share it with anyone... I'm not ready to explore those feelings. I hate her for what she did to me, for how she broke my heart... The girl I fell in love with... who fell in love with me... Maybe I can share that story... no I just want to get out of here with minimal damage and minimal sharing of my feelings and life.

The days seem to be getting better. I'm less angry, week three. I only have one week to go until my thirty days are over... though I have a feeling that thirty days here is not only a dream, but impossible. So the staff and other students say. Most kids seem to leave around week eight or nine. Some are here up to week thirteen. A record was eighteen weeks in the wilderness... fuck, I'm *not* going to be here that long.

On a completely different note, I'm the quiet one in the group. I'm usually the last to the fire in the morning and first to go to bed, sometimes I even go to bed before dinner. Except with the new staff I can't do that anymore. They want us to stay away for the nightly gathering.

A gathering is held at the fire after dinner. It is usually led by one of the staff. It can be a story or a lesson. Sometimes even a student leads the gathering. Most of the time I'm half asleep, so I don't get most of the message anyway.

Sunday nights we have goodbye gatherings, where we go around to the people who have been there the longest and share one good thing about them and one thing they can improve. It's incase they suddenly leave and we can't say goodbye, it happens a lot here.

Other news, a few other students have left our group and have been replaced by more of society's outcasts, a.k.a. us. I'm not really in the mood to elaborate on anymore of my experience... I'm so fucking exhausted of this place... this hell.

Day 23

I woke up at a new campsite, got my new food and prepared for my therapy visit.

I experimented with making bread today. With bananas in the inside, a Banana Pocket! It didn't turn out so well...

Right now, I'm alone at my own campsite, about a hundred yards from anybody else. This is called a "solo." I have my own fire, my own latrine and own sump. And I'm supposed to just reflect on life.

Oh and my parents are coming out here tomorrow. Joy... I can just tell them how much I hate their fucking guts... or I could convince them to take me home. I've been advised that that trick never works. But there is no shame in trying.

I've already cooked some ramen and macaroni. I'm about to cook some oatmeal, it's getting dark. For some reason I'm so hungry.

Day 24

I woke up with an intense pain in my stomach. It felt as if somebody stabbed me and I was dying. My nerves got the best of me and the two hours I was awake seemed unbearably long. I wiggled in the dirt, looking at the rising sun. I had an amazing view of the desert... the long barren desert.

From my campsite I could see the road and I could hear cars. The cars took like ten minutes to park 500 or so yards away. From the cars my parents emerged. Every parent visit requires the students to make a "Bull Roar." It's an Aborigine instrument made from wood that makes a sound when waved in the air. They were used to communicate with other tribes and if made right could be heard for miles. Different tones mean different things... Mine was kind of crappy.

After we finished the stupid Bull roar I watched as my parents slowly walked towards my campsite. I held back tears as I forgot how much hate and resentment had built up in me. My mom started running halfway there and I started laughing. It was impossible not to laugh considering I've never seen my mom run before.

And as much as I hate to admit it, I cried as she pulled me in her arms and hugged me. A mother's love and comfort is the best remedy when you're scared and alone. She was bawling. My dad walked up and pried my mom off so that he could hug me. They brought chairs for us to sit on... I got to relax in a chair for a few hours instead of sitting on a bluie or the rock hard ground.

We spent the day talking about where I was going after this and what's been going on in their lives. At this program there was a secret thing known as "tokens" that could be given.

To give a token, you take the person into a sacred area that is enclosed by rocks or tree branches or both. The opening to it faces east, allowing the morning spirits to enter as the new day comes in. Or some crap like that. In the center is a rock you place the token on or make a fire.

A token represents something another person sees in you. I gave both my parents the token of the "Winged Heart." It represents the courage that they showed throughout their lives, because I knew that both of them had experienced a lot of hurt and suffering.

I was giving the "Journey Keeper" token. I'm assuming because I'm always writing in this damn journal! The token represents someone who writes goals, sticks to them and keeps a day-to-day account of his life. Which is all me. It also represents a person that is driven.

After a few hours we had an hour therapy session and then the rest of the day was ours. Not much conversation went on after that. All three of us knew that it was just a matter of time before they had to leave.

Day 26

Today was the day that I received my trail name. A trail name is a name given to someone by the other students and staff. We go around in a circle, listing off adjectives to describe the person. Then we think of a noun such as an animal. Swift Wolf. Wise Mountain. Chirping Chick. You get the point? The names can be stupid. However it's a nice way to see what everyone thinks of you.

I was given the name "Rising Phoenix." Rising represents my constant setting of goals and then accomplishing them. I'm always "rising" above expectations and I'm always "rising" from my faults and miseries. The Phoenix was given to me partially because of my tattoo, but also because of who I am. I guess the other guys thought I represented immortality and beauty (haha). In all seriousness, the Phoenix also represents destruction and rebirth.

After the ceremony we waited for staff exchange, which happens usually around 2:00 PM (oh by the way, they don't let us know time, so we learn how to tell time by where the sun is in the sky. Every four fingers represents an hour. So 2:00 PM would be about six hands from the horizon) but they didn't arrive until 6:00 PM (basically just a few fingers from the horizon).

When the staff did arrive they told me to quickly pack my stuff and go to the road. We were recruited for a special group known as a "Boomerang". I was whisked away in a car with two other students from my group and two guys from another group. Without knowing what was happening, we sat in the car for four hours until we got to our destination. Apparently three female students had runaway from First Camp and they had trouble locating one of the students.

It was very dark by the time we reached our destination and we weren't exactly where we were supposed to be. Snow had blocked the road, so we had to hike with packs that were not hiking ready two miles up an icy road. Once we arrived at our destination we were extremely pleased. There was a teepee that we slept in and we had a port a potty! This was what First Camp was supposed to be, however a storm had broken the teepee and the roads were blocked by ice and snow. I guess it's our job this week to restore First Camp!

Day 27

This is a "leadership boomerang". We are supposed to learn leadership stuff. I didn't feel well today. I had a mini panic attack and my nerves caught up with me again. After a little while I was better and rejoined the group. It was cold and snowy today but we managed to set up our own shelters.

We also played a few games. One of which I really enjoyed. It is called Commander and Tank. Basically you have a partner who is blindfolded and you have several baggies full of bark lying around. It is the commander's job to direct the tank (the blindfolded person) to the baggies and to pick them up and throw them at the other tanks.

The rest of our day consisted of riddles and readings from books. We had two staff, a male and a female. The guy was a bit feminine with long hair. He was tall and nice, kind of quiet. The other staff was an outdoorsy female. She was funny with dry humor and came off bitchy. We got along really well.

She read from the <u>Tao of Pooh</u> and it was interesting to listen to the stories from one of my favorite childhood cartoon came from.

Day 30

Yesterday we had to leave First Camp (I'm assuming because our job was done and they were expecting the new students coming in to be there). We moved about a mile from where we were and set up camp.

Yesterday I was challenged to do many things I was not comfortable doing. I was to build another student's shelter and he mine. And the first night we were not allowed to adjust it in any way shape or form.

I lasted the night, but it sucked because he didn't like building shelter's the way I did.

I have trust issues. Hopefully you can see why. With the way my dad deceived me into coming here... by the amount of heartbreak I've experience in relationships. And by the torment I endured in middle school. I don't trust anyone. And to make matters worse shit hit the fan.

I received a letter today from my parents. Apparently one of my friends was arrested for shoplifting. And I was her accomplice. Well, sort of. A week before I came we stole two pairs of jeans together, one for her and one for me. Though I didn't physically take the jeans out myself, I knew what she was doing and the stolen jeans were going to be for me.

To make things just a little worse, the jeans I had worn out here (they are sitting in the office back in civilization) had been stolen as well. I borrowed them from my friend, and she had stolen them. They were actually really cute and even the staff complimented me on them when they escorted me away from my dad. They were True Religion Brand Jeans with gold horseshoes on the pockets... Oh how I hate to have to give those back!

Anyway, in a letter to my parents I had admitted to everything I had done and even shared with them things I didn't tell them previously. Except for this small little detail. Now they don't trust me. They think I'm lying about everything. Oh and they asked for all my passwords to all my accounts and found more things in my e-mail and on my MySpace. Things that they thought more of than they actually were.

I have no idea how I am suppose to defer this one... in the next few days I have IQ and psychoanalyst tests then I have a meeting with my education consultant. She is going to help assess me to figure out what kind of boarding school I should attend... great, more hell even when this is over.

Day 32

Today I woke up to see an empty space from main camp. A shelter was once there... the shelter of my best friend while out here. Apparently he left early this morning. He was one of my closest friends here in the wilderness. Anyway I don't care, I'll probably never talk to anyone from here ever again!

The whole point of this boomerang was to learn leadership skills. Staff members who thought we were in the right place in our program chose us to go on the boomerang. So that's what I'm going to do!

After breakfast I had the meeting with my Ed Consultant and things went well. Evidently not many actually come out into the field to meet the students. I was a special case. The staff cannot say enough good things about me. I guess I am a good manipulator, considering that if they actually read this stupid journal they'd know the truth.

After she left we decided to go on a day hike. We packed the little dry food we had (I had none, so I packed my powdered cheese and my spoon... it's very disgusting but at the same time the salty goodness from it just amazes me).

The hike was long (probably like nine miles), but we didn't have our packs. I carried my Possibles bag and we climbed up the mountainside. Once on top we walked a good distance along the ridge. It was absolutely stunning, the view. I hate the wilderness and the outdoors and the mountains and everything that's not the city. But this, I admit, was gorgeous.

When we came to the end of the ridge we entered into waist deep snow. I watched as two other students horsed around, pretending to be skiing and jumping trees. I was cold and hungry and just wanted to get back to camp; but it was hilarious to watch as the staff and other students got stuck in the snow!

Once we got back to camp we cooked a large dinner, getting rid of the rest of our food (well most of it; tomorrow is food drop, so we really don't care much if we don't have a lot for breakfast).

Day 33

Today we left the boomerang and headed back to the Dingos. When we arrived back into camp, minus one member, a whole new crew of students greeted us. The entire group had changed (and not for the better). From what the previous staff had said, there was another PB incident. The worst part, it was when the Dingos played a game that resembled lacrosse with the other group. A Dingo stole the PB from someone in that group! Great, I'm in a group full of troublemakers. Our new staff was an odd combination as well.

We had the redneck cowboy who was kind of cute, but in a way not. The second staff was a hippie with a beard. The third an awkwardly weird ex-firefighter? I think that's what he said. He was a big environmentalist though and boy did it get on my nerves! The fourth was an elf-looking guy with long hair and a moustache (March was Moustache March, so all the male staff members grew out a moustache). He was small and very girly.

I was given the leadership position in my group. It was my duty to help coordinate camp chores, and help keep everything moving smoothly as we set up and break down camp every day. I was honored that the staff felt I was a good enough leader for this group!

Day 36

Today we had an awesome change in luck! The elf-man got sick and went home. He was replaced with a teddy bear man named Dan. Dan brought Tabasco sauce with him for our meals and it was one of the most fantastic tastes ever!

We had a long hike and actually couldn't find our bluies. We were in the right place, but the ERV (emergency response vehicle) dropped it off a mile away. So we worked as a team to bring the bluies to our campsite.

The camp we made was very close to the road, less than the required 200 yards away, but it had a pre-existing fire pit. You see, out here everything we dig, we must fill back up. Our latrines must have at least six inches of space above our shit. Our sumps must have juniper braches to catch food, and then we have to burn that sump

catcher. Our fire pit coals have to be crushed, and then we use metal Billie cans (tin cans with holes punched in them) to sift the ash around. Anyway, a pre-existing fire pit means we don't have to sift the coals and ash!

Next to the fire pit was also a structure made from Juniper branches. It was supposed to be a sweat lodge. A sweat lodge is a small structure covered with tarps and sleeping bags. Inside is a pit where very hot (like it would sizzle your skin, hot) rocks are placed. Once inside, everyone sits in a circle and water is poured on the rocks after the entrance is shut. After a few minutes it becomes like a sauna and you sweat. It's very common among Native American cultures. It's very relaxing.

Tonight we heated up rocks and relaxed in the sweat lodge. It was a nice way to reward ourselves after a long hard hike.

Day 44

So two nights ago everyone decided not to build shelters, because it was a beautiful cloud-free night. Instead they just used a "burrito" style shelter. A burrito is where you wrap yourself in the large tarp. I was the only one to build a shelter. Not even the staff built a shelter. Well guess what... it snowed two inches. So everybody's belongings were covered in snow! We didn't have to hike that day!

Well last night, nobody made a shelter again. Thinking "it couldn't possibly snow again." Well it snowed again! And I was the only one with a shelter! I got a kick out of the whole situation because that's two days in a row that it snowed and everyone but me suffered because of it!

Day 45

So yeah, I've been here for nearly fifty days and decided just to throw out my self made calendar. I seriously don't think I'm ever going to get out of here! I've proven to be an effective leader though! And I've made seven Possibles Bags; a pair of flip-flops for around camp and made a lot of progress with my parents.

I've learned how to cook most delectable foods... though I still wish I had better food! I invented the "butter pocket," a delicious piece of butter bread with powdered butter in the middle. When the butter is heated up, the moisture from the bread causes the powdered butter to turn into a real butter substance! But be careful when using powdered butter. It is HIGHLY flammable. If you toss it into the fire, the fire seriously ignites like an explosion!

Butter Pocket Recipe

½ a baggie of Wheat Flour

1 handful of powdered butter

3 pinches of baking powder

¼ a baggie of Water (add more as needed)

Once you make the dough, place it on Billie can and put lots of powdered butter in the center. Fold the dough over the powdered butter, set the Billie can on the fire and let cook. It may take ten to fifteen minutes to fully cook.

Day 47

This morning I woke up and the staff hinted that I needed to be prepared to pack up and leave camp. So as everyone else was off making something with a special guest staff, I packed my things and prepared for my departure.

I was picked up by a group of people that had members I knew and members I never saw before. We hiked about three miles before setting up camp and waiting for the new staff. We had the old man, Buzz, the lanky ex-firefighter (great...) and a pretty young woman. She definitely became my favorite staff after she squealed at one of my jokes.

Day 48

Another boomerang... yay... Today we started out with a lovely hike. And by lovely, I mean I thought I was going to die. Or hurt someone. Or both. Six miles. Six fucking miles up a fucking hill.

When we arrived into camp a staff member said something to me that set me off. I started cussing him out and when another student tried to calm me down, I told him to fuck off. This is the first time in the seven weeks I've been here that I've shown anything other than compliance. I blew up and told everyone to fuck off. I told them to leave me alone.

I had a rough hike. I wasn't in the lead anymore and it showed. I have no idea how it happened. Afterwards, I spoke with another student and he commented on how out of character it was of me. And it was.

Day 50

Two more damn hikes. Eight more miles each. Sixteen more fucking miles up and down. Up and down. The pathway was ridiculous. It was like an obstacle course. My legs are soar and I had trouble keeping up with the other students. Best part, there was a road that was probably five miles long that led to the same place. (We went bird's eye of four miles, but with the hills it made us walk a distance of eight miles... stupid mountains).

Day 51

Today we rested and just chilled at our therapy site. It was very peaceful here. I talked with my therapist today about what was going on and she gave me a list of options (of boarding schools). I picked my favorite, but also said I'm ready to get out of here. So I told her whichever would take me first, I'll go to. I still have to be accepted by one of these stupid schools... meaning I'm going to be here just a tad bit longer.

Day 53

I was almost certain that I was supposed to leave yesterday. I didn't. I'm so fucking tired of this place! I just want to go home.

Today we went on a day hike, a hike that none of us wanted to go on. It consisted of us collecting Willow (a type of tree that grows like a weed and spreads like a disease as long as water is around). We also collected Ghost Beads.

In the ancient Australian culture, Ghost Beads represented a way to get into the afterlife. Ghost Beads are little shelled seeds from the Juniper berries that rodents chew on and take out the seed. The little hole is perfect for threading a string through (but you first have to make a hole on the other side).

Once you've done that, the story is that you must have 101 Ghost Beads to get into the afterlife. Each bead is given to a god; there are a hundred gods. However, the Wolf god is tricky and gets in line a second time, that's why you have to have an extra bead.

I collected 101 beads and made a bracelet out of seventy of the them for my favorite staff member and used the other thirty-one in a bracelet for myself.

Day 56

Today was an eventful day. I was taken from the Boomerang and placed in another car. I was going home... but wait no. I wasn't. I was placed with seven other individuals and we were driven to the edge of where we had been the last eight weeks. And we hiked.

We began the hike with a challenge, we were to not talk. This would later become a problem, because even when we took a break, we still couldn't talk! Every hour or so we would stop and take a ten minute break. This is where we ate some food, adjusted our packs and relieved ourselves.

Things got bad as the sun went down. We were still hiking and it was getting cold. We took longer breaks with shorter distances walked. Finally, as the staff said we were close, several students sat down and said they weren't going to move anymore.

We tried to reason with the staff to let us just camp here for the night, but they insisted that we keep going. We finally hit a road and walked along that. We didn't have to hop any more barbed wire fences for a while.

Again, another student decided to quit. I was determined to get there and refused to sit. I calmly explained to the other students that we had to do this. And after giving a compelling leadership speech, we continued on. I definitely felt like I made up for the past few days when I was behind everyone, and flipping out. Now I was the strong leader in the front with a calm manner about him.

After another thirty minutes we made it to our destination. We saw a giant teepee, a port-a-potty, and little ewok houses (so we called them). We claimed our new homes and we were excited about not having to build a shelter, sump, latrine, or fire pit (there was already a fire pit as well!).

Before bed, they sat us down for a quick gathering. We talked about rewards and hard work; and for the hard work and perseverance we just showed, they gave each of us a very large can of peaches… I'm not sure anyone can ever understand how delicious the peaches tasted and how incredibly awesome this place was in comparison to the rest of my experience in the wilderness.

Day 57

I am in Transition Camp. They don't like to tell us a lot, but I have the feeling this is the last phase of my journey here in the wilderness. And thank God! I am so over this place it's not even funny!

We have a lot of quiet time to ourselves here and we can literally just lie around in the sun all day. There isn't any more snow and it's so nice. The sun warms my skin as I lay in shorts and a cut off T-shirt. Every so often they ring a bell or make a sound with a didgeridoo and we have a gathering or eat lunch. Each of us is assigned to prepare a gathering.

Today we learned about the "Johari Window." The Johari Window is a concept of a window that is divided into four panes: A, B, F, and U. Each represents something about yourself.

Arena- the place everyone knows about you	**Blind spot-** what others see in you or know about you that you don't
Façade- What you know that other's don't because of a front you put on	**Unknown-** the things that neither you or others know about yourself

My Strength Circle (what my peers said they saw in me)

"You know who you are and what you want to do"

"I feel you are extremely strong"

"Motivation and Determination"

"Productive"

My Improvement Circle (what my peers said I could improve)

"Be more open"

"Pride is thinking your self-worth depends on the things you do and it is a false foundation for your real self worth"

"Don't let your history be an obstacle to your future. Let go"

Day 58

I was almost sure that this morning was when I was supposed to be discharged... but I'm still here. I talked with my therapist today and she informed me that mom had to have a minor surgery, which delayed my discharge. This fucking sucks. I'll probably be here another week or so.

Today we took a little hike up a large hill and played "what's in my square". We had to draw what we saw in our one foot by one foot pretend enclosure and describe it.

"It's a plateau. With a little valley below and a small forest. It's like a small sanctuary. Blades of grass cover most of the area but there are spots of rock and soil."

This was supposed to make us stop to look at the smaller things in life and to appreciate what was there and how we can benefit from not always looking at the big picture. The biggest lesson I've learned is that life is not about where I end up but the journey I take.

After our little lesson we played a game of baseball with a bat that another student carved and a ball made from leather filled with rocks and rice. My team won both games!

After our fun game of wilderness baseball, we were each placed on a solo where we were to reflect even more on our transition. This was our time to be alone... sadly I knew I wasn't leaving like everyone else...

I'm not sure if I'm going to just stay here in T-Camp until Monday… cause I'm pretty sure that's the date. Ninety-nine percent sure. Well I guess I'm going to just cook a bunch of food and then sleep.

Day 59

They sent me back to First Camp (which is actually right by T-Camp, you can literally hear the other camp... which is why I guess they asked us to keep our voices down at T-Camp!)

Today I'm still on solo and will remain on solo until further notice. I'm very bored and really don't know what I'm going to do to make this next week pass by.

Day 61

I was taken off of solo and joined the ranks of First Camp. However, most of the students at First Camp were actually from group. There was a cute girl with a boot on her foot (from injuring herself in a hike, I'm assuming) and another on safety/run watch. Both are talkative. It's nice to interact with the opposite sex again.

Today I invented a new recipe. All I had was tuna, Germaid and some spices. I hate tuna but a staff gave me the idea of making a tuna patty (like a hamburger) using the Germaid as filler to hold the tuna together. After careful planning I concocted the most amazing recipe.

Wilderness Tuna Patty Goodness

1 packet of Tuna

¼ a baggie of Germaid

2 pinches of Mrs. Dash seasoning

½ of a Lime

1 pinch of Salt and Pepper

Put the tuna packet into a baggie and add the germaid. Mix until solid. Add lime juice and continue mixing until all the dry germaid is packed with the tuna and is wet. Mold into a patty (must be solid form). Put a Billie can on the fire and let it pre-heat for a few minutes. Take the Billie can off and quickly add Mrs. Dash on top. Place the tuna patty mix on the Billie can and put back into the fire. Watch carefully as it cooks fast. Flip the patty. You can add carrots, broccoli and/or celery at your discretion.

Day 62

Today I was swept away to T-Camp once more. This time the girl with the boot joined me. Her name was Jay. She was cute and funny, though the staff encouraged us not to talk too much to one another.

Day 63

I have never heard a girl fart as loud as Jay... and then giggle even louder! She has been a real comic relief in my situation and we get along very well. Today we found a bin next to the port a potty full of trash. The trash consisted of a soda bottle, tortilla wrappers, marshmallows and other junk food.

I took the bag of uneaten marshmallows and a two-liter bottle of Pepsi back to my shelter and Jay and I shared the delicious junk food treats. Later that night the staff admitted that he saw some goodies in there and went to get some. Well since we had already took them, they obviously weren't there and we were busted. We returned the half gone bottle of Pepsi and told them that we ate the entire bag of marshmallows. We got a good laugh out of it (at least Jay and I did!).

Day 64

So I've been thinking. I had a conversation with the boarding school (on the landline that I mentioned) and I realized something. My goal was to graduate from high school early and this boarding school requires me to commit to one year. I was absolutely furious and devised a plan to get out of it.

I spent a lot of time and drafted several letters and possible solutions before concluding with this letter…

Mom and Dad,

I feel that this school is *not* the right school for my future goals and ambitions. It requires a one-year commitment, has non-transferable credits and no self-paced classes. As you know I was to graduate before I turn eighteen.

In all honesty though, I don't want to go "home." Plano isn't my home anymore. I feel both betrayed and abandoned by my friends and family. I consider the west desert, middle-of-nowhere more of my home. With that in mind, you can see that this is hard for me.

Option one: go to this boarding school, be prevented from excelling and graduating early and being stuck on campus there at eighteen years old.

Option two: find a way to go back to Plano, face the people I can't trust and not really know what on Earth I'm going to do.

This is the beginning of being completely honest and open with you, like y'all wanted. I have brainstormed many options, some of which involve me going back to Plano and a few which could get me out within a month or two.

I refuse to be imprisoned past the age of eighteen. Going to this school and leaving when I turn eighteen will cause me to forfeit my high school diploma. My education is very important to me right now. I don't want to give up my high school diploma (or the equivalent).

If you read this and I'm not here, I'm sorry. I will talk call you soon.

All my love

-Steven

Day 65

It's breakfast time and I am writing as my food is cooking. I'm cooking a large baked potato, a large loaf of bread, and oatmeal... I'm starving... Oh jeeze... I hear cars... the staff is insisting it's probably just wood... it stopped outside. I think I'm leaving!

* * *

April 20th

This is the last page of my story keeper. I want to take this page to share all I've learned. Coming to the wilderness program made me very angry. I saw this as a punishment; a punishment that was unfit for the things I did.

My parents, to me, were nothing more than objects. I used tears and anger to manipulate them into getting what I wanted. I also lost sight of who I was and who I was becoming. Lying, stealing, drugs and sex became my everyday life. I lied to my parents about who I was with, where I was going and what I was doing.

I stole expensive items for the rush. I experimented with ecstasy and smoked cigarettes without any shame. I skipped class because I just didn't care. I put aside my books, my scripts, dreams and goals just so I could party. I was content with it too. Or was I?

I had lost myself and gave up searching. I really wanted to go back but it was easier to not face the truth. I have worked on my trust issues and I'm working on forgiveness and selflessness. I've come such a long way and everyday I see a little more change.

I've struggled to just make it each day. This is a challenge that I wake up to every morning, hoping it will just end. But then I remind myself... what doesn't kill me will make me stronger. And I'm still alive.

The length of this journey was unknown to me but now it's over and I can begin a new chapter in my life.

-Rising Phoenix has spoken and he has been heard-

Day 66

I've been banned from having a journal, pens, paper and the like. I'm on run/safety watch. I'm back in First Camp. Oh, I forgot to mention, I've been sent back to the wilderness program... less than twenty-four hours after my discharge... I'm pretty sure it's a record here.

I was given a small story keeper from one of the staff, though my therapist has suggested that I not be allowed to have one. What she doesn't know won't kill her, right? Let me try to squeeze the past twenty-four hours into this small journal.

The staff pulled up and brought one bag of laundry. Either Jay or I was leaving... the staff went to talk to the transporters and I looked at the laundry bag. It had Jay's name on it... meaning I was leaving. Jay started crying and I gave her a big hug and assured her she was leaving in two days... I knew the exact day she was leaving because I figured the schedule of program out. You go to T-Camp on a Friday and leave the following Wednesday. Wednesday was discharge day for the program. But they made an exception for me. I got to leave on a Monday.

After I was discharged, my parents greeted me. I took my first shower in nine weeks, shaved, and even got to put on deodorant! I was still a little grimy, but let me tell you I have never felt better (physically) in my life. My teeth are extremely white (all the staff commented on how white they were, asking if I bleached them... as if I could bleach them in the wilderness!). My parents gave me a pack of gum and a Dr. Pepper... my first Dr. Pepper in nine weeks... I about cried because of the satisfaction the simple taste gave me... time seriously stopped.

From the office we drove to McDonald's and that began my eating spree before I was off for boarding school. I had a quick snack (nuggets and fries) and quickly finished the delicious grossness as we pulled into Chili's for lunch. There I consumed even more food. (The majority of my time out was spent eating, it's hard to explain how much you appreciate food when you don't have to cook it, and it's different than what you've been eating for the last nine weeks.)

We went to the grocery store and loaded up on everything from Oreos to Goldfish to candy. We were staying at a nice hotel in Park City (the place where they had the Olympics that one time a while back.) This was probably the best day in my life, considering the circumstances. I was discharged, ate all the food I could dream of, got my hair cut, showered, and I was treated to a manicure/pedicure for my gross hands and feet.

After a lovely dinner at Ruth Chris steakhouse, we retired for the evening. This is when things got sketchy. It was about 11:00 PM when I decided to sneak out to the computer lab. I took my dad's debit card and tried to log onto my accounts. I found out that my parents deleted all of them. Furious, I went to the closest gas station (across the street) to buy a pack of cigarettes. Of course after nine weeks they were absolutely disgusting and threw the pack away.

I went back to the hotel, grabbed the rental car keys and took off. I drove around and finally stopped at a Burger King and had a midnight snack. I pulled into a parking lot and ate my food. Before I took off I left a note for my parents (the one I described in my previous journal). I shut the bathroom door and turned on the shower before I left, to give them the impression I was still there... well I planned on them not realizing I was missing until it was too late to stop me (a.k.a. 7:00 AM in the morning).

My plan to return the rental car, take money from my dad's debit account and buy a bus ticket out of Utah was foiled when a police officer pulled into the parking lot next to me, asking me to leave the vehicle. My parents realized I took the car and reported it stolen immediately.

I began panicking and crying and the officer was kind and calmed me down before my dad arrived. When my dad arrived, he gave me a choice: either go to jail or come back to the hotel without a fuss with him. I was too pretty to go to jail... I'd be somebody's bitch in no time, no doubt.

So I went back with my dad. The next few hours were spent with my mom crying, my dad yelling and my poor little brother in the other room trying to sleep with the madness I had created.

Because of the "runaway" attempt, my parents called the wilderness program and they expressed their disappointment and informed us that the boarding school probably won't accept me now. After almost no sleep we woke up to return everything we bought the previous day for the boarding school.

I missed my opportunity and all the signs... how could I have been so blind. My dad assured me and looked me straight in the eyes and promised me I wasn't coming back... that he didn't want me back in the wilderness... I had to pee when returning the things we bought and my mother asked me "Do you need someone to be in there with you?" I asked "Are you planning on sending me back to wilderness?" and she simply said no... so I didn't run... I didn't fucking run because I trusted that my parents wouldn't put me back there... I served my time, paid my debt. I trusted that we'd figure something out.

At noon we had a meeting with the people from the wilderness program... okay... it was to discuss what we can do to fix this situation since I refused to go to the boarding school... well, if that wasn't enough of the sign... I complied.

While in the office we sat and we talked. After telling me I was going back out into the field, the man and my dad left the room. I sat there, crying, begging my mom to not make me go back. I begged for forgiveness and pleaded... but the decision was already made. I clung onto my mom, the comfort her hugs gave me... then the man came back in and my mom had to leave.

That's when I completely lost it. I started screaming and throwing a fit, threatening them... they asked me if I would go calmly... I insisted I wasn't going back... and they said they could use force... force? What the fuck?! What kind of force are we talking about here anyway? Like beating me up until I do what they say? Sedating me?

My pleads went unanswered. There was no other option. My parents didn't want me... there were no other placement options... I was sentenced to an unknown time back in the wilderness, without any place lined up... I could be here forever, I thought.

I can't believe my parents lied to me again... I just didn't want to go to that boarding school, I wanted to be normal again. I turn eighteen in a matter of months; I just want to spend my remaining time free before becoming a legal adult... but what... no. I swear to God, if there even is one, that I am packing my bags the moment I get home and those mother fuckers will never see my face in person again. They will never hear my voice directed towards them. They will never, and I mean never have a relationship with me again. I don't even hate them. It's worse. I'm indifferent to them. With hate, at least there is a feeling there. With hate, there's a chance that someone can turn it around... no this isn't hate. This is full blown indifference.

So... with puffy eyes, and tears blurring my vision I complied. I went through the procedure once more. I didn't have to get a physical this time though. I begged for anything to comfort me... my jacket. No. My jeans. No. My Burt's Bees. No. Please just my Burt's Bees... Fine. I smiled. I actually smiled because I was allowed to take one thing with me. My Burt's Bees lip balm. My tears cleared up and I was placed on run/safety watch. A beautiful young woman named Olivia sat with me the entire time and hugged me, talked to me... she made me feel better.

Even when we showed back at First Camp, she sat next to me until she had to go, just talking to me... And here I am. Back in the beginning... It's harder the second time because the shock of what you're going to be doing isn't there... just the shock of leaving and being back here twenty-four hours later.

Day 69

Some argue that my time here started over when I came back, but I refuse to think of this day as day one, again. I was gone for twenty-four hours before I came back and I'm continuing counting my days in the field, consecutive or not.

Today I left first camp to join the Dingos once more. The group was completely different. I recognized only three faces from the seven other students. I'm still on safety/run watch. It's hard to hide my notepad and storykeeper from the staff (though I'm not sure they really know I'm not suppose to have them).

My therapist explained to me why I wasn't allowed to keep a journal when I came back. She told me that I hid behind it. I write all my thoughts down so I don't feel the need to share them with anybody. She also referred to my drawings as a way to "escape" my situation. And it's true. My journal was the only thing that made the time pass by. I don't know how long she will keep me from getting a new composition notebook… hopefully not long at all. She wants me to open up more to the group. Until she caves, I'll have to make due… writing extremely small… in the margins…

The New Group

(For their privacy, their names have been reduced to the first initial)

C: He's quiet. I actually saw him in first camp. He came the day before I left for T-Camp round two. He's quick to lose his temper, but he seems to have a lot of insight. I think he's here by choice, or something like that. He knew he was going to be here apparently. He actually called the wilderness program from the airport when he couldn't find them.

K: He says he's straight-edge (no drugs, alcohol or sex) with the exception that he has a lot of sex. He's a womanizer. He reminds me of me. It's very strange. He's arrogant and always thinks he's right. He doesn't like to hear that his way is the wrong way. Just like me. Or at least how I was. Of course I'm still arrogant, a bit of a narcissist, and don't take no for an answer... but seeing it in him, I realized that I've definitely changed a little bit.

T: He's very quiet... and shy. Timid. He reminds me (and everyone else) of the little son in The Munster's. I don't like him very much... and it seems nobody else does either.

A: He's loud, obnoxious and tiny. He's very outspoken and rude.

The other three were in the previous group so I know them... I really don't like any of them very much.

Day 73

Today I got into a yelling match with my therapist. She demanded I hand over my notepad. I refused... however eventually I gave in. But only because I knew that I had my mini-story keeper that she doesn't know about. I intend to keep it that way too.

Day 76

One of the other students left today. Instead of hiking with our packs, we were able to take a day hike to the peak of a mountain nearby. It's called Red Pine. It's a very tall mountain. The day started off smoothly. We had a little more time at breakfast to cook since we wouldn't be having a warm lunch.

After everybody got ready... after we did the required pulse checks before hiking (a measurement the staff use to determine if we are hydrated enough) and everyone passed, we began our day's journey.

The beginning of the hike was easy. Very subtle climb uphill. We would stop for a break every now and then to enjoy the view. Because it's about the journey, not the endpoint. The day was warm in comparison to my previous stay. There were only patches of snow remaining. I wore shorts the entire hike.

Our first long break came after we went on a very hard hike uphill. The angle of the mountain was almost a ninety-degree angle from the ground. We waited as T (remember I'm using first initials only) slowly made his way up.

C, K, A, a staff and myself managed to make it further up. About half an hour later one of the other students came up to us and asked us to come down. We argued for a while but eventually we went down to see what the hold up was.

T had decided this was "too hard" and wouldn't move. C, K and I went back up and decided we were at least going to get as far as we could. I mean we were literally one more ten-minute push to the top!

Our goal was to pee off the top of the mountain as a group (it may not make sense, but it's one of the most exhilarating moments.)

To keep to that goal, we peed off of the side of the mountain where there was a ledge. After doing so we talked about how awesome the feeling is. And how it must suck to be a girl, because only guys can experience this rush... well actually we figured out a way girls can get the same, if not a better one.

First, the girl must do two things: 1) Makes sure she has a buddy and 2) take her pants off all the way (a number of tragedies could occur if the pants remained on). The girl and her buddy must walk to the edge of the cliff and face each other.

They must lock hands tightly (only one hand is required, the other hand can be thrown in the air to thrown up in excitement). The girl peeing must then squat and pee while the buddy balances her by pulling her back to keep her from falling. At this time both the girl and her buddy must scream "woahhhhhhhhhhhhh!" very loud. Mission complete.

Anyway, back on track. After peeing off the mountain, T refused to go any further and the staff made us go back to camp. None of us were happy campers (no pun intended). T decided to stay at his shelter and nobody thought of him as we began to prepare for dinner.

Twenty or so minutes later I had to use the latrine and on my way back I noticed I didn't see him hanging out of his shelter like he was when I passed by earlier. I thought nothing of it. After washing my hands with the stupid camp suds I sat down by the fire. From our camp we could see the road clearly. A car was driving along and it stopped.

Dinnertime. The staff called for T, but no response. I pointed out my observation earlier of how I didn't see him at his shelter, and I heard movement in the woods. Then I pointed out that that car we saw had stopped. The staff discovered that T had indeed become a runaway.

After an hour or so of searching, T came back with a staff member. Apparently he had turned around when he realized he didn't know where to go. He even mentioned that a car had offered him a ride but was scared the man was a sexual predator or murderer (in the middle of nowhere, what are the chances of that? I sure as hell would have taken him up on his offer!).

T was placed on run/safety watch (the first person other than me that I witnessed to be placed on it since I first got here).

Day 78

Today we hiked through a park. It was weird, a bunch of rednecks in RVs... 200 miles away from civilization (or at least 200 miles from the program's office... maybe there is a city closer... other than Dugway Military base).

Two girls followed our group chasing their dog that was "running away." They brought us otter pops, however the staff wouldn't let us take them. So we had them "drop" the otter pops without the staff seeing. Very carefully, one of the other students picked them up after I told him where the girls dropped the otter pops. They were absolutely delicious... and better yet the staff didn't have a clue!

Day 80

So the dumb ass of the group decided not to crush the coals from his solo fire and he literally set the forest on fire. It cleared a good twenty or so yards. Of course now we have to help put it out... and call the ERV... and delay our hike.

I know I'm not writing much... but my paper source is limited. Hopefully you're enjoying the pictures I've included... each one kind of expresses the day I drew it.

Day 81

I will never forget today. I don't even think amnesia can rid me of this memory.

It started off as a very mellow day. A mellow hiking day. During breakfast it drizzled, but by the time camp was cleaned and our packs were ready, the sun was brightly shining. I decided to change my clothes. I put on my shorts, rolled up my short sleeve shirt, and packed my rain jacket.

We began the hike. One of the staff had loaned me a book, <u>Einstein's Dreams</u>, which I absolutely fell in love with. I seriously couldn't put it down. During the hike I read it, well tried to... while walking with forty pounds on my back, it was definitely a struggle. So I refrained from reading while we hiked and read on breaks.

We stopped along the road when we reached an area filled with hundreds of cattle. Cows, bulls and calves all filled the prairie. With the exception of the staff, T and I, everyone took their packs off to chase the cattle around. Their goal was to slap at least one on the ass (which K insisted he did).

Now this is when it gets memorable. You remember the part about me changing my clothes? And packing my rain jacket? And the brightly shining sun? Yeah well, about three miles into the hike we began our ascent up Indian Mountain (I believe the tallest in the area). The hill we walked up was probably a thirty-degree rise.

To make sense of how memorable this hike was, it began to drizzle. And then the drizzle turned into rain… pouring rain. And it got very cold, very fast. As we continued up the mountain it began to hail.

After an hour of hiking we stopped in a forest area… everybody was soaking wet… covered in mud. The trail we were taking was dirt, so of course the entire trail was now slippery mud. We waited for a staff and T to catch up. We waited at least fifteen minutes before starting again.

The rest of the hike consisted of us struggling to stay up while hiking with forty pounds on our backs in the slippery mud, while freezing cold in the hail with very little clothing on.

Once we got to camp everything was soaked. We set up our shelters so we could change. My fingers were so numb I couldn't even tie up my shelter. I seriously had a melt down because I was trying so damn hard and it just wasn't happening. C had partially set up his shelter and offered it so I could get into warm dry clothing. I took him up on his offer and soon after completed my shelter. I crawled into my sleeping bag and waited until I was summoned... I was "changing" when they came to get me... not sleeping. Shh.

The sun eventually came out right before it set. It was out for maybe an hour, it warmed us up. It took us almost two hours to bust a coal to get a fire. The wood in the area was absolutely soaked, making it hard for a nest to go into flames, and adding wood to make the fire, very difficult. Luckily we were settled by sun down.

Day 82

New staff. A very queer man that reminds me of a leprechaun and a boyish girl are here to lead us this coming week. Is all the female staff manish? The female staff member understands my journal and has given me more paper! Yay! I was almost out. Though I think the fire-crotch staff may know I'm not supposed to have it, the way he keeps looking at me as I am writing.

Day 83

Another day hike! They are giving our group another chance after the stunt T pulled!! We are hiking up Indian peak!! I'm very excited... partially because I hate moving campsites and hiking with packs.

There wasn't anything really interesting to tell about this hike except that I found a pair of deer antlers and once we got to the top there was a water bottle full of paper that past groups have signed and put little notes in. So everyone in our group joined the tradition.

Day 84

Today I was supposed to give a gathering... I was incredibly nervous because it's a topic I've never openly discussed with anybody. Many of my friends know parts of this story, because they witnessed it. But nobody knows the full story. To everyone here at the wilderness program, I'm gay. Until tonight when I went into detail about my life.

"I wrote a life story when I first got here... but it was from a skewed, pissed off bias. I skipped over probably the influential parts of my life so far.

I played with dolls and dressed up in my mom's high heels when I was little. I liked girly things, and wasn't into sports. I was very creative and liked to draw. All my life I've been out of the ordinary.

When I was two, my parents divorced and my "new mommy" stepped in and raised me when my birth mom wasn't there. All I can say about those relationships is that it is a very hard subject, a very touchy subject. I am extremely lucky to have moms who both love me with all their hearts and want what's best for me. But it's a catch-22... they both love me, but they both fight for my love. Neither will accept that my love for each is equal.

It's a very tricky line that I have to walk. Always watching my words... always making sure I don't accidentally call one of them by their names or refer to the other as mom. It's tough.

I moved around a lot until we came to Texas in 2000. I always resented my parents for moving on my birthday, in the middle of the year. I especially hated that they made me leave all my friends. For once in my life I didn't feel different, but we moved and I started over.

I guess it started in fifth grade when I started praying to God every night that I wouldn't turn out to be gay. I started praying because people had started calling me names… even parents. I was too queer to be straight. I tried playing soccer. I was good at it, but hated it and soon quit.

Middle school came and the rumors poured in. I didn't have many friends but everybody knew who I was. People would whisper things about me as I walked by. They tripped me and "bumped" into me. Just little things like that. I finally told my parents about it and they called the school.

After several meetings with the dean, the principal and the counselor all of them "tried" to contain the issue. But nothing helped. They didn't issue discipline or even call their parents. My dad had enough and actually went to someone's house and talked to his dad (without me knowing.)

As it continued, we persisted with the school. I came home crying… I cried at school. I was being tortured verbally. I had people who would stand up for me, but they faded out as the rumors continued. My parents actively called the school, but nothing was done about it.

At the end of my sixth grade year I thought it would be better if I just killed myself. I tried cutting my wrist with my nails. Scratching until

I bleed... then scratching even more, and more... but I couldn't do it. I just couldn't do it. I went to counseling but stopped going after a few months.

Seventh grade rolled around and things continued to escalate. People pushed me and threw things at me. Every morning I dreaded walking into the cafeteria, knowing at least twenty people were staring and whispering about me. What did I do to deserve this?

I became very involved in church and God. My faith was the strongest it had ever been. I was the lead in a musical mission trip. I attended church two to three times a week. I did everything that a "good Christian" did. And I believed in God with all my heart. I had to. It's honestly the only thing that kept me from killing myself during this harassment.

I continued to pray every night that I could just be normal. That I didn't have to be gay. I never really thought of guys before these rumors started, but as I started puberty I did take an interest. I got sexually excited at the sight of a "hot" guy. Don't get me wrong, I got boners by looking at naked women as well... but this gay thing was... is so exciting because of the taboo. But, I prayed that I wasn't gay. I denied it. I wouldn't let myself become gay. I made remarks that all gay people should be killed; that they didn't deserve to live. Those comments came mostly from my family's influence on me. How I acted towards the issue was horrible.

As the seventh grade continued it got worse and worse and worse. The administration did absolutely nothing. My parents worked so much to help me but nothing seemed to be working. Finally at the end of the year, my parents withdrew me from the school and I was going to start a new school the next year.

After a decent eighth grade year, I fought a very hard fight. The school all my new friends were going to was a "closed" school. Meaning they didn't accept transfers. The only school I could go to was the high school that everyone that I hated went to. The exact crowd that made middle school hell.

They denied my transfer request. I had to go and register and enroll in the school with the people that made me want to kill myself. I got my schedule... I took my picture... I saw everyone I had ever hated...

My dad wrote a letter to the school board. You have to understand that my parents were very close to taking the case to court. Against the school, the school board and even individuals. They were willing to go to court and file charges of slander and deprivation of character on my behalf. I never fully appreciated it. I took it for granted because I was so angry and so depressed. Well after my dad's letter, they accepted my transfer request... a week before school started.

Now, let's go back a little to my seventh grade year (I was twelve). I remember it so perfectly... I was playing a character "Casey" (From the poem Casey at the Bat) and my best friend at the time introduced me to this girl, her friend. We will call her S (anyone who knows me will know who it is, but again, privacy). S had a crush on me and she thought I was cute. To this day she insists that was the first time we met. I have a different memory.

We were on a church outing. Bowling. It was my two best friends, S and me hanging out. After a very fun night of playing arcade games and bowling, we got back into the bus. S had used her tickets to get a thing of flavored lip-gloss and we sat together, flirting, and tasting the lip-gloss... weird, we're aware.

Pretty soon we decided to be boyfriend/girlfriend. A concept so farfetched while someone is that young. For the next two years we were on again/ off again. We talked all the time, we hung out all the time... we became each other's best friends. For my fourteenth birthday we went to see <u>Christmas with the Kranks</u>. It was our first official date together and it was the first time we kissed. It was electrical. I was her first kiss (though she wasn't mine).

We had both fallen in love with each other. Very soon after she decided she couldn't "handle" a relationship. Nothing new in our world... except this time it was actually over... at least it felt like it. I didn't speak to her for nearly a year, but when we did speak again none of the feelings I had for her went away. She admitted the same. We dated again and my fifteenth birthday came. Happy Birthday! She broke up with me on my birthday weekend.

A few months later we rekindled the broken hearts and we took our relationship to another level. We explored the sexual realm of the relationship and again she decided she didn't want to be in a relationship as "intense" as ours. Meaning she was scared of love... at least that's how I interpreted it. I found out soon after she was seeing another guy, and I hit the rebound. I was in the middle of filming a movie (I was casting actors the day she broke up with me) and the movie made for an easy escape.

The movie I made was based on my experience with bullying. It followed a documentary about high school cliques. I spent nearly eight months working so hard to make this movie work. My parents were less than supportive, they didn't believe in me. But I still managed with a zero dollar budget, at age fifteen. After filming was done, the editor told me his computer crashed and he had to start over with editing... a month later he sent me a nasty e-mail insulting my competence and the way I made the movie.

Keep in mind, he was twenty-three, much older. He refused to hand over any footage. Looking back now, I figure he lost most of the footage we filmed when his computer crashed. Though he couldn't admit to it after all our hard work and long hours. I quit film, I quit acting, and I quit writing. Everything that I was good at, I just quit.

Meanwhile, I cut off communications again with S again. The next summer I met a guy over the Internet who told me he thought I was cute. After getting to "know" each other on the Internet, we decided to meet in person. I asked my lesbian friends to join us on a double date, and they did. That night I kissed a guy for the first time.

When my parents found out that I met him in person, they flipped out and I promised I wouldn't talk to him again. For the next year I committed to that. I slowly started talking to S again. We became really good friends once more and I even went to Africa with her family over the summer for ten days. While there, we spent some of the nights out by the pool looking at the stars talking to each other, we even kissed.

But again, she said she couldn't do it. After I turned seventeen I decided to explore the stuffed away sexuality that I feared. A month later I was "out" and told everyone I was gay. I labeled myself as gay because since I was eleven years old people have called me gay, faggot, queer, etc. It was easier this way. It was easier to just go along. Every time I denied it there were certain people who kept on saying "You're gay, just admit it." And I couldn't admit it because I didn't know. But I went with it. Fuck it, I don't care anymore.

I told my parents in hopes that they would kick me out, but they didn't. They hate the idea of it, but worked very hard to accept it... well they tried to accept it. I'm not quite sure they have yet... But they are trying to do what they believe is best for me, even if I don't see that."

The group seemed to be interested in my story and asked me a lot of questions… it made me actually feel good about where I was for the first time in nearly twelve weeks. Well I'm off to bed now… I feel really good about sharing my life story with them...

Day 85

New site. It's Sunday night, so therapy is tomorrow. You know... when I came back I was told they didn't know how long I'd be out here for this time around. I was thinking anywhere from a few days to maybe two weeks. It's been twenty days now. I'm hoping to leave soon, but honestly I'm just not quite sure it's going to happen.

I can't stand my parents. They haven't really written me any letters, other than "we're working on your next placement." They aren't filling me in on details and I feel locked in the closet. I just wish that they would consider what I thought this time. I would like to graduate but I'd be fine with a GED.

I hate to admit it... but I'm actually enjoying it here. This time around, the group is actually full of people I can trust and people who will listen to me. We've started constructing and using showers.

We usually shower on Monday or Tuesday. The weather is mostly warm but we still build a fire by the shower to heat the water.

How do you make a shower in the wilderness? Good question. First you take tarps and set them up as a wall to block the wind/give you some privacy. Part of the tarp covers the ground to keep your feet clean. Second, you have a fire going and you pour water into a Billie can and put it on the fire. You have to remove the Billie can and then use the camp suds and scrub-a-dub- dub! And rinse. And finally you can use the shampoo and conditioner that (if you're lucky) the therapist brings out with her. Ta-da!

We set up camp in a very nice location. We are planning on making a sweat lodge, and we spent today digging it into the ground, cutting down tree branches, and the like to build it.

I got lucky when it came to locations to put my shelter. K and I found an area with very soft white sand! K built a shelter that he actually had to dig; it was pretty tight.

Day 86

Okay so I would have wrote this last night, but a situation came up. A came over to talk to K and me and we started discussing the best way to run from the program and it just turned into a "plan" on how we would do it. Long story short, the staff overheard us. Well, all three of us are on safety/run watch.

It was really all my fault for starting it. They both seemed to be supportive of it though and I bet if we would have tried it we could have been the first in the history of the program to escape! Or at least it would have been a cool story.

So here I am, sitting on my little tarp in the open, while the staff figures out how to maintain three students on run watch while at the same time keeping up with the other part of our group.

Oh and the staff were so angry that we won't be able to do the sweat lodge we were planning to do...

* * *

So I talked to my therapist. She was extremely angry but at the same time she seemed very calm about the whole situation. She also seemed to have a vague idea of my next placement but wouldn't share any of the details with me... bummer.

I also asked for a composition notebook but no such luck. She told me that she was actually considering giving me one until I "pulled this stunt." Yeah, sure she was.

It's all right; C offered me one of his composition notebooks and asked for a new one. So now I can start writing in that one. I'm seriously on the last page of this story keeper.

Day 88

I woke up this morning with K and A next to me. We're on watch, so we all have to sleep with the staff and honestly, it's very crowded! The three students and the three staff (they called in for help of another staff.)

By breakfast time, A was transported out of the group along with two other students. Now all that remained was C, K, T and myself. A very small group, the smallest I have ever been in my entire twelve weeks out here!

During our hike we got two more students, we can call them students B and D. B is extremely tall and very quiet where as D is short and very loud. They came from another group and have been here for a while (probably like four weeks).

Day 90

Never thought I'd write that day down when I first got here... the time sure has flown by! When a staff member has been out in the field for a total of hundred days they get a little patch that says so. And the same for 200 hundred days. Of course, it's easier being a staff because they aren't a hundred days straight! I wonder if I am out here for 100 days, will get a hundred day patch or not? I think I deserve it. Even if it's by my doing, it's still a hundred days in the wilderness, right?

A few days ago on our hike T was put on watch along with K and I... half of our group is on safety/run watch. So when we got to our new site, the staff made us make two separate camps. One for the "good kids" and one for us. We had our own fire and our own sump. It was pretty ridiculous. But whatever.

We had staff exchange yesterday and we got a whole bunch of cool staff. We have a guy that looks like Obi Wan Kenobi, the girl from my second boomerang (the one I gave the bracelet too), another chick and a kind of quiet guy. Great detail, I know!

When we woke up this morning we were expecting a group of trainees to join us and when they finally arrived it was cool. They were absolutely ecstatic to be there and were amazed that I had been in the field for 90 days.

Day 91

Today was a special day for me. I decided to give a token to one of the staff members that I had a connection with. I set up the Bora Ground and got the pigment for painting her face. It was a unique experience, giving someone something like that. I can't really explain what it feels like.

When you give someone a token it's because you have seen something in that person (it's not a reward). And you're showing him or her that you noticed it. When you leave the Bora Ground it's an amazing experience knowing someone has seen a change or seen something special in you.

Day 93

Last night was one of the most amazing experiences of my time here in the wilderness. As a group we went on a night hike. There are now only five students and we had four staff plus the four trainees. We set off after the heat of day (it reached nearly ninety degrees) and the hike was mostly on the road.

At one point during the night we saw the wild horses that migrate through this area. They were quite a distance away, but we still got the feeling of amazement. I even turned to one of the staff and said "If I took my pack off and starting running towards the horses, got on one, and started riding away, what would you do?"

She laughed and said "I would yell 'Go Steven! Go!" Another staff laughed about how the phone conversation with the ERV would go. "Uh... we have a runaway... he's heading towards the main road on a wild horse." It was pretty hilarious.

The best part of the entire hike came when the sun began to set. The sky became a bright pink and purple frenzy. The air cooled down and it was relaxing. Since it's Sunday, we held our goodbye gathering at one of our breaks. I was the first to stand up in front of everybody as they said good-bye to me.

They told me how creative I was. How I managed to keep the spirits of the entire group up with my bubbly personality. They applauded me on how I keep my cool even though I have been out here for almost fifteen weeks, not knowing what's going to happen because I fucked up. And how I help everyone with their issues and listen to their problems. I'm a survivor.

I was told to let go of my arrogance. Sometimes I walk around like I know better than the staff (which is debatable since many of the staff were hired after I started the program). They told me to just trust my gut and not second-guess myself.

After an hour or so we continued on. We could hear coyotes howling at the full moon. We stopped to howl back. The full moon was beautiful. It provided us with light and it was a bright white color. When we got into camp everything was calm and clear so we just threw down a tarp and fell asleep under the stars (I'm still on watch, so we still had to sleep with the staff).

Today we had a "spa day." We set up an extra sump so that we could wash our hair. The pretty female staff was in charge of washing our dirty hair.

Day 99

Before we left camp this the morning I stated that I wanted this last hike to be memorable because I know it's my last hike. The hike, like every hike, started out sunny and well but then we hit the base of a mountain, a very steep mountain that we had to climb over to get to our campsite. Well, little did we know there were about five other hills we had to cross of about the same steepness.

Once we made camp, three hours later, I sat down to think to myself. I planned a ceremony for my group members to honor the time we've spent together. I decided to make a special Bora Ground for my team. I used fire to burn symbols into wood tokens with a meaning behind each of them. Knowing this was my last Sunday (don't ask how I know, I just have a feeling I'm leaving sometime this week) I thought it would be a nice goodbye thing to do with a group that I had opened up with so much.

Day 100

Wow... 100 days in the wilderness... I'm in disbelief. Today really sucked. It poured last night and everything was soaking wet when we woke up. All of our fire sets were wet, the wood we collected and even the bark on the trees. Luckily we had some dry bark in a baggie. After we assembled a group shelter we dug another fire pit. Then it started raining.

We took a break until lunch because after several hours of trying to bust a coal, we couldn't do it. Not even tandem (where two people bust a coal together.) Well, we could bust a coal some of the time, we just couldn't blow it into flames. We each just lied in our shelters eating our dry food and reading or writing.

Our therapist was supposed to be arriving anytime, but she was nowhere to be found. At lunchtime we tried another round of busting but no luck. Then the rain started pouring really hard and we even heard thunder. We gathered in a circle, huddled up to keep the bark for our nest dry along with our dry fire sets.

"Some times in our lives. We all have pain, we all have sorrow..." I began to sing and everyone gradually joined in as we sang "Lean on Me" to keep our minds from wandering. Pretty soon the rain let up and after trying to bust a coal tandem we finally did it and blew the flames into fire! That's when our therapist arrived.

We actually talked about the possibility of her being a witch. Every time she came out here the weather was extremely beautiful. Even in an instance like this when a thunderstorm hovered above not even ten minutes before, it just goes away when she shows up.

Day 102

I woke up this morning expecting to see the transporters... no such luck. I went to breakfast like normal and talked with C and K. I seriously thought I was leaving today. It's Wednesday, if not today then one more week... I don't think I can handle another week here. I'm ready to move on.

I've already packed all my things ready for today's hike, so I'm sitting here waiting for everyone to do the same. One of the other students got sick last night and I think the staff are trying to take care of him. Anywho, I guess I'll just doodle until their ready.

It has been a roller coaster being here. I still remember when I first came, when my parents decided to send me here. I told them I had to work. They grounded me on Valentine's day so I wasn't allowed to go out and I just wanted so bad to hang out with someone. My week consisted of losing my cell phone Saturday, getting a smoking ticket Monday, getting a red-light ticket the same day, my mom thought I lied to her about where I had been and took my car away from me, I was grounded on V-Day, then Friday came. Instead of actually being at work I went to hang out with a friend.

I have an anti-theft system on my car and my parents shut my car down after calling my work and finding out that I wasn't even scheduled. I found a pay phone and call them, distressed because I had gotten lost and was in a bad part of town and my car wouldn't start. I promised I'd be home... I didn't show up until almost two hours later.

My dad told me we were going to grab a bite to eat; I just wanted to clean my messy room. On our way I noticed we weren't going anywhere close. He told me we were going to airport to eat. Then when we got there he said we were going to Salt Lake City. He mentioned something about a conference (the following week we were suppose to attend a seminar thing about parents struggling with their child's homosexuality.)

The next morning we sat in the lobby waiting for someone to pick us up. He told me that we were going to look at some "facilities." As they were walking in my dad said that I'd be going alone. I asked how long and they said about thirty to sixty days. I said okay, I could do thirty days.

As you can see, I was caught off guard so much that I couldn't even fathom what was happening. I didn't know where I was going. I couldn't fight back because I didn't know what I was fighting against. I just cried, in disbelief.

When I first got here and learned what the program was looking for in an "ideal student" I quickly put my game face on. I did all my assignments, therapy and school credit. I didn't give the staff grief, and after a few weeks I actually became very helpful and motivated.

After my parents' visit and my meeting with my Ed Consultant, I got discouraged about leaving here in the thirty days I first clung onto so badly and made a goal of six weeks. Well the Ed Consultant shattered that hope when she said it could take three weeks to get me in somewhere. Seven weeks I can do this.

I went to T-Camp, eight weeks down. Then my discharge got delayed because of my mom's surgery. I was looking at nine weeks out here. That's when I decided that I didn't want what we had discussed (my parents, therapist, Ed Consultant and me).

Twenty-four hours later I was back. This time I didn't care about the time frame. I could leave any day and by picking a specific date it made me unhappy. I started living each day as it came and man did that make a difference in my life.

I have a new outlook on life. I use to have every detail of my life set. This is what I'm going to do by this age. I'm going to be making this much a year... etc, etc, etc. But the lesson I learned and value most is to live each day as it is. It could be my last. Instead of knowing everything, I accept that I would rather just do everything I can without obsessing about tomorrow. Because this moment is all I'm guaranteed.

And even though I'm bummed I'm still trying my hardest to just hang in here a little longer... oh my God...

I left that day. It was a bittersweet moment. I was pumped to go but at the same time I really didn't know what was going to come next. I didn't know exactly where I was going and I was comfortable with where I was. I had become accustomed to living in the wilderness.

My greatest accomplishment, no matter what I may achieve in the future, is the conquering of my worst fear. If nothing else is gained from this experience, at least I can say I'm not afraid to be lost. I'm not afraid to be alone. I'm not afraid to not know everything. I'm not afraid to trust. I'm not afraid to forgive. And above all, the greatest hurtle in all this was my own mind. But I'm not afraid of myself anymore. I survived myself, Steven.

Ven Rey

The journey I took during my wilderness expedition was unexpected, forced and intimidating. However it has changed my life forever. No longer am I afraid of new things, challenging things

"Veni. Vidi. Vici."
-Julius Caesar

www.ingramcontent.com/pod-product-compliance
Lightning Source LLC
Chambersburg PA
CBHW032129090426
42743CB00007B/527